IMAGES OF WAR

TANKS & ARMOUR AT LENINGRAD 1941–44

RARE PHOTOGRAPHS FROM WARTIME ARCHIVES

Ian Baxter

Pen & Sword
MILITARY

First published in Great Britain in 2026 by
PEN & SWORD MILITARY
an imprint of Pen & Sword Books Ltd
Yorkshire – Philadelphia

ISBN 978-1-03612-259-1

Typeset by Concept, Huddersfield, West Yorkshire, HD4 5JL.
Printed and bound in England by CPI Group (UK) Ltd, Croydon, CR0 4YY.

The Publisher's authorised representative in the EU for product safety is Authorised Rep Compliance Ltd, Ground Floor, 71 Lower Baggot Street, Dublin D02 P593, Ireland – www.arccompliance.com

For a complete list of Pen & Sword titles please contact
PEN & SWORD BOOKS LTD
47 Church Street, Barnsley, South Yorkshire, S70 2AS, England
E-mail: enquiries@pen-and-sword.co.uk
Website: www.pen-and-sword.co.uk
or
PEN & SWORD BOOKS
1950 Lawrence Road, Havertown, PA 19083, USA
E-mail: uspen-and-sword@casematepublishers.com
Website: www.penandswordbooks.com

Contents

About the Author

Ian Baxter is a military historian who specialises in German twentieth-century military history. He has written more than seventy books, including *Poland: The Eighteen-Day Victory March*; *Panzers in North Africa*; *The Waffen-SS Ardennes Offensive*; *The Western Campaign*; *The 12th SS Panzer Division Hitlerjugend*; *Waffen-SS on the Western Front*; *Waffen-SS on the Eastern Front*; *The Red Army at Stalingrad*; *Elite German Forces of World War II*; *Armoured Warfare: German Tanks of World War II*; *Blitzkrieg*; *Panzer Divisions at War*; *German Armoured Vehicles of World War Two*; *Last Two Years of the Waffen-SS at War*; *German Soldier Uniforms and Insignia*; *German Guns of the Third Reich*; *From Retreat to Defeat: The Last Years of the German Army at War 1943–45* and, most recently, *The Sixth Army and the Road to Stalingrad*.

He has written over a hundred articles, including 'Last days of Hitler', 'Wolf's Lair', 'The Story of the V1 and V2 Rocket Programme', 'Secret Aircraft of World War Two', 'Rommel at Tobruk', 'Hitler's War with his Generals', 'Secret British Plans to Assassinate Hitler', 'The SS at Arnhem', 'Hitlerjugend', 'Battle of Caen 1944', 'Gebirgsjäger at War', 'Panzer Crews', 'Hitlerjugend Guerrillas', 'Last Battles in the East', 'The Battle of Berlin' and many more.

He has also reviewed numerous military studies for publication, supplied thousands of photographs and important documents to various publishers and film production companies worldwide, and he lectures to schools, colleges and universities throughout the United Kingdom and the Republic of Ireland.

Prelude

At dawn on 22 June 1941, along an 1,800-mile-long invasion front, 3 million German soldiers on the frontier of the Soviet Union unleashed one of the most brutal conflicts of the twentieth century – Operation Barbarossa. For the invasion of Russia, the German Army assembled 3 million men, divided into a total of 105 infantry divisions and 32 Panzer divisions. There were 3,332 tanks, over 7,000 artillery pieces, 60,000 motor vehicles and 625,000 horses. This force was distributed into three German army groups. Army Group North, commanded by Field Marshal Wilhelm Ritter von Leeb, had assembled his forces in East Prussia on the Lithuanian frontier and would provide the main spearhead for the advance on Leningrad, consisting of 812 tanks. These were divided among the 1st, 6th, and 8th Panzer Divisions, 3rd, 36th Motorised-Infantry Division and the SS Motorised-Division 'Totenkopf', which formed the Panzer Group reserve.

Leeb's Army Group North was given the task of destroying the Red Army fighting in the Baltic region. Hitler stipulated on the eve of the invasion that the German objective was for his powerful armoured spearheads to thrust across East Prussia, smashing Soviet positions along the Baltic, liquidating the bases of the Baltic Fleet, and destroying what was left of the Russian naval power and capturing Kronstadt and Leningrad. Once the city had been razed to the ground, the German armies could sweep down from the north while the main force closed in from the west. With 500,000 men at Leeb's disposal, comprising almost thirty divisions, six of them armoured and motorized with 1,500 Panzers and 12,000 heavy weapons, plus an air fleet of nearly 1,000 planes, he was determined to strike along the Baltic coast and destroy the Soviet's Army in the North.

For the Russian offensive, the Panzer divisions had been slightly modified in armoured firepower. They had been, in fact, diluted in strength to form the deployment of more divisions. The planners thought that by concentrating a number of Panzer divisions together, they could achieve local superiority. These new Panzer divisions contained one tank regiment of two, sometimes three Abteiliungen totalling 150–200 tanks; two motorized rifle (schützen) regiments, each of two battalions, whose infantry were carried in armoured halftracks or similar vehicles, and a reconnaissance battalion of three companies (one motorcycle, two armoured car). The motorized infantry divisions accompanying the Panzer divisions in the Panzer Group were similarly organized but severely lacked armoured support. The divisional artillery comprised of two field, one medium and one anti-tank regiment and an anti-aircraft battalion. These were all motorised and more than capable of keeping up with the fast-moving Panzers. It was believed that these modified armoured units were the key to success in Russia. Using his armour to spearhead the first attacks during the morning of 22 June 1941 Leeb launched a rapid two-pronged offensive along the Baltic. His force consisting of 16th and 18th Armies quickly smashed through the Soviet defences.

The armoured strength of the 16th Army comprised of the LVI Motorised Corps with the 3rd Motorised Infantry Division SS-Totenkopf, XXXIX Motor-ised Corps which was made up by the 12th Panzer Division and 20th Motorised Infantry Division, Panzer Group 4 which included the Polizei Division, XXXXI Motorised Corps which comprised of the 1st, 6th, 8th Panzer Division, and 36th Motorised Division. The bulk of the armoured force comprised mainly of the Pz.Kpfw.I, II, III and IV, the Pz.Kpfw.35(t), Pz.Kpfw.38(t) and the Sturm-geschütz (StuG) assault gun. The Pz.Kpfw.III was the primary main battle tank in the summer of 1941 and the most common Panzer at the start of Operation Barbarossa. The Pz.Kpfw.IV was also a significant tank, but during the initial stages of the war on the Eastern Front it was more of a close-support tank until it was later upgraded with a longer 7.5cm gun. The Panzerwaffe relied heavily on the Pz.Kpfw.III and for the invasion, the Ausf.G to Ausf.J variants of these tanks featured 30mm thicker frontal armour, offering greater protection.

In addition to the tanks, each Panzer division had gained a motorized infantry regiment. This had increased the division's operational ability to gain more ground quickly and attack urbanised areas more effectively, protect its flanks, sweep up bypassed centres of resistance, hold positions, and often successfully counter-attack. Off-road mobility was also enhanced as the number of halftracks increased as the firepower was further supplemented by the addition of assault guns and anti-aircraft battalions to the Panzer divisions.

As for the 18th Army, its armoured strength was minimal and composed of infantry divisions using armoured vehicles primarily for support, reconnaissance, and transport, rather than as the division's principal offensive force. For the invasion of the Soviet Union, the average frontline German Infantry Division had about 1,000 motor vehicles, around 600 of them being trucks. Some subunits of these divisions were often fully motorized, such as the Signals, Anti-Tank, and Reconnaissance Battalions. The backbone of these vehicles in the Reconnaissance Battalions comprised of the Schwerer Panzerfunkwagen Sd.Kfz.263 8 Rad Heavy Armoured Radio Car, the Schwerer Panzerspähwagen (Fu) Sd.Kfz.232 8 Rad Heavy Reconnaissance Radio Vehicle Sd.Kfz.232, the Schwerer Panzerspähwagen Sd.Kfz.231 8 Rad Heavy Armoured Reconnaissance Vehicle Sd.Kfz.231. There was also the Leichter Panzerspähwagen (MG) Sd.Kfz.221 armoured car.

For transporting personnel to the front lines, the infantry divisions widely used the Sd.Kfz.251 halftrack. Halftracks were of prime importance in the German arsenal, relying on vehicles such as the Sd.Kfz.6 which was used for towing ordnance such as the 10.5cm leFH 18 howitzer. There was the Sd.Kfz.7 which was a special purpose vehicle used as a prime mover for artillery. Other prime movers included the Sd.Kfz.8 for towing heavy guns such as the 21cm Morser 18, the

17cm Kanone 18, and the 10.5cm FlaK 38. A very popular halftrack in the summer of 1941 was the Sd.Kfz.10 which was a special motorized vehicle. Its main role was a prime mover for small, towed infantry and Luftwaffe guns such as the 2cm Flak 30, the 7.5cm leIG, or the 3.7cm PaK 36 anti-tank gun. The Sd.Kfz.10 was unique and versatile among the halftracks and there were many variants which included mounting a flak gun on the back of the vehicle known as the Sd.Kfz.10/4 and 10/5. There were other field modifications made which included fitting the 3.7cm PaK 36 or 5cm PaK 38 anti-tank gun.

For the opening of the attack into Soviet Union during the early morning of 22 June 1941, the 4th Panzer Group advanced in two spearheads led by the powerful XLI Panzer Corps and the LVI Panzer Corps. Their objective was to drive its armour across the Neman and Daugava rivers and head for Leningrad. In front of the German armour stood the Soviet 3rd and 12th Mechanized corps who were given orders to outflank the Panzers and prevent them from driving east. By the evening of the first day of the attack the German armoured spearheads were over the Nieman and had driven over 50 miles. The next day near the town of Raseiniai, the XLI Panzer Corps was counterattacked by the 3rd and 12th Mechanized corps. Supporting the German armoured column was the Luftwaffe from Luftflotte 1 which immediately attacked the Soviet tanks south-west of Siauliai. The aerial attack was intense and precise, and many Russian armoured vehicles were destroyed. However, despite the German armoured columns being well-protected by air cover, the 6th Panzer Division, composing of 114th Panzer-grenadier Regiment (motorized infantry), Aufklärungsabteilung 57 (Panzer Reconnaissance Battalion 57), one company of Panzerjäger Battalion 41 and Motorcycle Battalion 6 were attacked by the Soviet 2nd Tank Division from the 3rd Mechanised Corps near the town of Skaudvile. What followed were Panzers and Russian tanks including the Soviet KV-1 and KV-2 tanks fighting fanatically with the Soviet units trying to contain and destroy enemy armour and troops from crossing the Neman River. However, coupled with excellent fighting tactics and the overwhelming strength of the Germans, the Soviets were unable to prevent them advancing. The result of the battle was the first major tank battle that took place in the early stages of Barbarossa. The fighting saw the destruction of the majority of the Soviet armoured forces of the Northwestern Front. The outcome, referred to by the Soviet Army as the 'Border Defensive Battles', saw German armour and supporting infantry heavily attack towards the crossings of the Daugava River.

Even though the Northwestern Front had been mauled in the fighting along the Baltic border, Soviet commanders ordered their remaining troops and armour to slowly fall back. Whilst the border battles were costly in men and material, the Soviet forces managed to avoid any major encirclement. They effectively succeeded in delaying Army Group North in order to sufficiently allow its Soviet forces time to prepare for the defence of Leningrad. Many of the soldiers who had participated in the operation were rerouted to defend Leningrad or the Moscow Front. A tactical withdrawal followed, but it was not continuous, it was interjected by brief counterattacks, counterstrokes or counteroffensives.

Chapter One

Battle for Leningrad

By 2 July, the 4th Panzer Group completed its regrouping on the Dvina and ordered its armoured columns towards Ostrov, which fell to 41st Panzer Corps on 4–5 July. The Panzer Corps then swung north eastwards at speed towards Pskov, which was heavily defended by the 1st Mechanised Corps from the Leningrad Military District and 41st Rifle Corps. However, the 1st Mechanised Corps lacked sufficient armour from the 1st Tank Division, and its 163rd Mechanised Division had received heavy losses during a counterattack. The only tank division which was at almost full strength was the 3rd Tank Division.

On 8 July the 41st Panzer Corps supported by the 1st Infantry Corps advanced on the town of Pskov and despite Russian resistance, the town fell in a couple of days. Whist the 41st Panzer fought for Pskov, the 56th Panzer Corps advanced from through Ostrov with the objective of making a wide sweeping flanking attack towards Novgorod and Lake Ilmen.

During early July, both the German 16th and 18th Armies quickly achieved tactical success despite some areas of heavy Russian resistance. In many areas, Soviet soldiers often stood helpless in the path of the overwhelming German strength. Although the fighting was punctuated by various Soviet counterattacks which stalled German armoured columns from their rapid advance, through July, armoured vehicles of Army Group North continued to smash through enemy positions heading straight towards their objective – Leningrad. Fortunately, the earth was baked under the blistering summer heat and Leeb's army rapidly advanced.

By 10 July, Leeb's units broke south of Pskov and rolled toward Luga. At the rate they were advancing, they would need no more than nine or ten days to reach the outskirts of Leningrad. But following their surge of success, the Wehrmacht were losing momentum. Not only were their supply lines being over-stretched, but enemy resistance began to stiffen on the road to Leningrad. In a desperate attempt to blunt the German advance and prevent them from reaching the imperial city, brigades of Russian marines, naval units, and more than 80,000 men from the Baltic Fleet were hastily sent into action against Leeb's forces. These Russian soldiers were now the sole barrier between Leningrad and the Germans.

Fortunately for the Baltic Fleet, German Army Group North was vastly over-extended. Its forces had advanced on a wide front and were operating in a number of independent outflanking drives with the sole intention of destroying the enemy in front of Leningrad. In fact, in order to achieve the destruction of the Russian forces, he required thirty-five divisions, but only had twenty-six. As a result, Panzers were overstretched and despite supporting infantry attacks, they were unable to take Kingisepp and Narva on 17 August. They also encountered very strong opposition around Luga. By 20 August, German forces reached Chudovo and destroyed the main rail link between Leningrad and Moscow which helped prevent further military suppliers reaching the Russian front in front of Leningrad.

Although the German advance had been overstretched and hampered by Russian resistance, by the end of August 1941, Leeb's Panzers were finally within sight of Leningrad. Assisting Army Group North achieve its objectives were Finnish forces who were operating north of Leningrad. The main objective of both the German and Finnish forces was to encircle Leningrad and maintain the siege perimeter, which included severing all communication with the city and preventing the Soviet forces who were defending the city from receiving any suppliers. The Finnish Army was creating a siege position from the Gulf of Finland to Lake Ladoga, with the main objective of eventually isolating Leningrad from all directions.

In front of Finnish forces was the Soviet 'Northern Front' which had a primary objective of the defence of the Kola Peninsula Kola and the northern shores of the Gulf of Finland. On 23 August, the Front's forces were divided into the Karelian Front and the Leningrad Front. The Front comprised of the 7th Army, 14th Army, 23rd Armies and the Leningrad People's Opolchenive Army. Other units were composed of four Rifles Corps, two Mechanized Corps, seventeen Rifle Divisions, four Tank Divisions, two Motor Rifle Divisions, eight artillery regiments of Highest Command, eight Aviation Divisions, seven Fortified Regions, one Fortified Position, and thirteen machinegun battalions.

Supporting the Northern Front was the Northwestern Front which had been heavily embroiled in the Battle for the Baltics. During the first eighteen days of the German invasion of the Soviet Union the Northwestern Front had been pushed back over 350 miles east. By late August it had become pivotal to the fighting around Leningrad.

The military situation for the Russian Army looked bleak and the terrified civilians left within the city walls of Leningrad were now going to endure one of the most brutal sieges in twentieth century history. With reports of German forces drawing closer to the city gates, Leningraders were given the grim orders to defend their city to the death. Although Leeb's forces had arrived within shelling distance of Leningrad, the advance had not gone as planned. Units had already been badly disrupted and were mired on the Leningrad Front by stiffening resistance. Yet, in spite of this resistance, on 30 August the last rail connection to Leningrad was cutoff when German armoured columns reached the Neva River. Leeb was more than confident that Leningrad would soon fall after receiving reports of the evacuation of civilians and industrial goods from the city. Orders were immediately sent out to destroy the Red Army forces around the city.

With news that Leningrad was about to fall, on 15 September, much to the astonishment of Leeb, 4 Panzer Group was transferred to Army Group Centre along with the powerful 41st Panzer Corps. Leeb was required to sledgehammer his way to the outskirts of Leningrad and move to the Moscow Front. Without the 41st Panzer Corps, the whole dynamics of Army Group North had altered. There would now be no attack on Leningrad. Instead, Hitler ordered that the city would be encircled and the inhabitants defending inside would be starved to death.

During October and November 1941, some ten German divisions were tied down around the city. For the next year, the German troops of Army Group North fought a series of bloody battles to hold their positions around Leningrad. Although they had managed to blunt Russian penetrations through their lines with the sacrifice of thousands of men killed and wounded, the battle had in fact absorbed all the available resources of the 18th Army and elements of the 11th Army, which had resulted in the planned assault on Leningrad being abandoned.

A Pz.Kpfw.III advances across a field during the opening phase of operation *Barbarossa*. The Pz.Kpfw.III was the primary main battle tank in the summer of 1941 and the most numerous Panzer at the start of the attack in Army Group North.

(**Opposite, above**) A column of StuGs on the advance supporting infantry. The 18th Army totalled twenty-one infantry divisions, which comprised of five old Luftwaffe field divisions. There were no reserves and very little armour. It was the first time the Sturmgeschütz was given the primary role on a large scale in supporting troops on the battlefield.

(**Opposite, below**) A StuG.III can be seen in an infantry support role. The StuG had a crew of four and came equipped with a 7.5cm StuK 37 L/24 gun capable of traversing from 12.5 degrees left to 12.5 degrees right.

(**Above**) A prime mover can be seen hauling a 15cm field howitzer along a dirt track. These halftracks were mostly used as a tractor for heavy artillery pieces and were generally not modified for other roles apart from some numerous anti-tank conversions.

German infantry cross a river on an inflatable boat and pass a Russian tank that has been submerged up to its turret after the crew evidently misjudged the depth of the water.

A column of armour and support vehicles supported by air cover can be seen advancing across a field. Almost immediately when Barbarossa was launched, the Panzer divisions exploited the terrain and concerted such a series of hammer blows to the Red Army that it was deemed only a matter of time before the campaign would be over. Yet in spite of these successes, the Panzer divisions were thinly spread out.

Two Soviet KV-1 tanks concealed besides trees can be seen knocked out of action. The KV-1 tank was known for its heavy armour protection during the early stages of the war. In certain situations, even a single KV-1 supported by infantry could halt German formations.

A StuG.III in a field. During the early phase of the invasion of the Baltic and the Soviet Union the StuG proved its worth, especially clearing out enemy infantry in urbanized areas. However, because of its fixed turret, it was limited.

(**Above**) A StuG.III advancing through a field supporting infantry. In the distance, buildings can be seen burning.

(**Opposite, above**) A KV-1 tank can be seen knocked out of action next to a destroyed 8.8cm FlaK gun on its trailer. The KV-1 tanks were almost immune to the German 3.7cm KwK 36 and the short barrelled 7.5cm KwK 37 guns that were found on the early Pz.Kpfw.III and Pz.Kpfw.IV tanks. Until the Germans developed more effective guns, the KV-1 was invulnerable to almost any German weapon except the 8.8cm FlaK gun.

(**Opposite, below**) A German infantry man surveys the gun barrel of a knocked out T-34 tank. The T-34 was a Soviet medium tank. When introduced, its 76.2 mm tank gun was more powerful than many of the Panzers it confronted. The T-34 was a decisive part of the mechanized divisions that formed the backbone of the Soviet battle strategy.

A Luftwaffe prime mover with flak personnel can be seen hauling an 8.8cm FlaK gun towards the battlefront.

A variety of German armoured vehicles can be seen in a field comprising of Pz.Kpfw.IIIs and Sd.Kfz.10 halftracks. These halftracks provided additional support to the Panzer divisions during their advance through Russia.

The crew of a Soviet KV-1 tank have misjudged the terrain during what appears to have been quite a battle. It has fallen off the edge of a concrete structure onto its side, knocking itself out of action.

(**Above**) Finnish army using a captured Soviet T28 tank during the battle around Lapland on 8 July 1941. The Finnish army participated in the siege of Leningrad. Although they did not directly attack the city, they set-up defensive positions around the city instead. However, the Finnish army did advance within 15-miles of Leningrad's northern suburbs by August 1941 and moved through East Karelia, threatening the city from the east. (*SA-KUVA*)

(**Opposite, above**) During a pause in their advance, shirtless crewmembers can be seen with their StuG.III. Throughout the war the Sturmgeschütz crews never regarded themselves as tank men. Rather, they were artillerymen manning mobile assault guns.

(**Opposite, below**) The crew of a Pz.Kpfw.IV can be seen motoring long a dusty road. During the initial stages of the invasion of the Soviet Union, commanders in the field soon realized that only the 7.5cm gun of the Pz.Kpfw.IV were really suited to the demands of the modern battlefield. However, even this gun had its limitations. The short barrel gave the shells limited velocity, which was effective against thinly built enemy tanks, but proved far from adequate against heavier tanks.

An interesting photograph showing infantry and mountain troops or Gebirgsjager hitching a lift on board a Pz.Kpfw.IV. Throughout the entire campaign in Russia, due to the long distances in which foot soldiers had to march, troops often hitched a lift on various vehicles and then dismounted to regroup and go into action.

Russian vehicles have been abandoned by the crew after coming under heavy attack and can be seen knocked out of action in a river.

A Soviet T-34 has been knocked out of action inside a forest during intense fighting along the Estonian and Russian border in June 1941.

A Luftwaffe halftrack towing an 8.8cm FlaK gun can be seen advancing towards the battlefront during the early stages of the Soviet invasion.

A well camouflaged Pz.Kpfw.IV can be seen on a road during the first weeks of *Barbarossa*. A long column of horses hauling supplies move in the opposite direction.

A Pz.Kpfw.III can be seen at a rail hub ready for transportation on a flatbed rail car destined for the front lines. Each Panzer Division was fully equipped when they invaded Russia. Each division fielded two motorized infantry regiments with two infantry battalions.

A StuG.III hurtles along a dusty road bound for another position. The vehicles main task was to suppress heavy infantry and anti-tank weapons that could not be destroyed by heavy infantry weapons. During the first years on the Eastern Front, the assault gun proved indispensable to infantrymen and the elite Waffen-SS alike.

A Pz.Kpfw.38(t) can be seen rolling along a road towards the front. This light tank was used during the early part of the invasion of Russia but panzer crews soon found that Soviet T-34 tanks were superior as the 3.7cm PaK 36 gun was often incapable of penetrating the T-34's armour.

A Pz.Kpfw.II advances along a dirt track. Although this light panzer had originally been designed as a stopgap solution while larger, more advanced tanks were developed, it nonetheless went on to play an important role in the initial stages of the war on the Eastern Front.

A Pz.Kpfw.38(t) hurtles at speed along a dusty road. One of the crew members wears aviator goggles in order to help prevent dust in his eyes and help him with visibility.

(**Opposite, above**) A Pz.Kpfw.38(t) wades across a river. In the summer of 1941, the Panzer divisions relied heavily on the lighter tanks such as the Pz.Kpfw.38(t) to provide the armoured punch necessary to break through enemy lines. Consequently, by late summer this put an increasing strain on the light tanks, and as a result many of them were either destroyed or developed mechanical problems.

(**Opposite, below**) A Pz.Kpfw.II advances through one of the many forest roads followed by a motorcycle. Motorcycles were used in a variety of roles including patrolling, intelligence gathering, and police duties. Motorcyclists could be found in every unit of an infantry and Panzer division, especially during the early part of the war. They were even incorporated in the divisional staffs, which included a motorcycle messenger platoon. Their versatility enabled them to survey enemy positions until they encountered enemy fire and then return swiftly with important data and other pieces of vital information relating to the location and strength of the enemy.

(**Above**) A mobile maintenance unit can be seen removing an engine from a prime mover using a wood hoist. Special maintenance companies on the Eastern Front were pivotal to the operating success of German armour.

(**Opposite, above**) During a pause in the advance the crew of an Sd.Kfz.10/4 can be seen with their vehicle. The halftrack was undoubtedly the workhorse on the Eastern Front, especially along the terrible road system that plagued seemingly endless miles of terrain. Its effective towing capability ensured that troops and ordnance often got through unhindered.

(**Opposite, below**) Pioneers can be seen still erecting a pontoon bridge as prime mover crosses towing a 15cm field howitzer. Construction of pontoon bridges remained a vital asset, especially to heavy armour. A well-trained Pioneer Bridging Column could build a bridge often in a matter of hours.

(**Above**) A prime mover has halted along a typical dirt road in northern Russia. Behind the halftrack are two Horch Cross Country cars.

(**Below**) During an armoured unit's assault and an Sd.Kfz.7 can be seen pulling an 8.8cm FlaK gun across an open dusty field. The gun is mounted on the cruciform mount, which is itself fitted with Sd.Ah.203 bogie units.

(**Above**) A halftrack towing a 15cm field howitzer crosses a heavy pontoon bridge known by the Germans as a Bruckengerat B. The pontoon boats have been lashed together and the bridging deck sections secured over them to allow traffic and soldiers on foot to pass over.

(**Opposite, above**) An Sd.Kfz.10/4 armed with mounted FlaK gun can be seen in action against an enemy target. The hinged sides have been completely removed for combat to allow the crew plenty of space to use the gun and reload with ammunition. Anti-aircraft defences came into prominence by August and September 1941, as the Soviet Air Force started to inflict heavier casualties.

(**Opposite, below**) A Sd.Kfz.223 radio communication vehicle can be seen advancing along a road. This light reconnaissance vehicle was four-wheeled drive and carried an 80-watt FuG 12 radio set. It comprised of a three-man crew consisting of a driver, commander and radio operator.

A variety of armoured vehicles belonging to the 12th Panzer Division can be seen spread out across a field. In July 1941, the 12th Panzer was moved to the Eastern Front and took part in operations to encircle Minsk, cross the Dnieper and to take Smolensk. The division was then shifted to Army Group North, where it successfully fought in the Battle of Mga. However, by the winter suffered heavy losses during the Soviet Winter counter-offensive north of Leningrad.

An Sd.Kfz.251 armoured personnel carrier can be seen wading across a stream. Due to the success of this vehicle in the early war years, these halftracks were given a frontline combat role alongside the panzer on the Eastern Front. Note the Sd.Kfz.222 Panzerspähwagen (FU) radio car following behind.

A German infantryman surveys a knocked out Soviet KV-1 tank during Russian defensive fighting. This tank weighed 50-tons and because it was impervious to most anti-tank guns it could often prevent Panzer units from breaking through its defences, especially.

A Pz.Kpfw.IV can be seen halted during a brief respite in their unit's advance. During the initial stages of Barbarossa the Panzerwaffe became aware of the appearance of the Russian KV-1 and T-34 tanks that prompted an upgrade to its 7.5cm gun to a longer high-velocity 7.5cm gun which was suitable for anti-tank use.

A halftrack prime move hauls a 15cm field howitzer along a typical Russian road. Even during the initial stages of the invasion supply situation was exacerbated by the almost non-existence of proper roads throughout the Soviet Union. Halftracks and other tracked vehicles were utilized to help speed up the supply of ammunition and other equipment desperately required for the front.

An Sd.Kfz.6 with an artillery tractor body is ferried across a river. Note the engineers bridging ramps stowed for use as exit ramps once the ferry reached the far shore.

A column of prime movers towing 15cm field howitzers have halted in a town. The gun carriage was a split-trail design with box legs. Spades were carried on the sides of the legs that could be mounted onto the ends for added stability. The howitzer was designed primarily for horse towing, and because of this, it used an unsprung axle and hard rubber tires. Halftracks were often utilized for towing where possible to keep pace with the fast-moving armoured spearheads.

A captured Russian tractor pulls vehicles along a muddy road. For the Panzer divisions in Army Group North, mud was a formidable foe. The mud produced from a few hours of rain was enough to turn a relatively typical uneven Russian road into a quagmire

A prime mover towing ordnance to the front. Despite the numerous types of halftrack in the German arsenal, the Panzerwaffe did not provide enough vehicles for the ground forces on the Eastern Front, with the bulk of the infantry being moved on foot. In fact, only about half of all units in Russia were motorized. Generally, ordnance was hauled by draught animals.

A Finnish soldier can be seen standing next to a captured Soviet T-28 medium tank during winter operations. This tank was deployed during the Russian war against Finland in 1939. Captured tanks were then used by the Finns on the Leningrad Front against the Russians. Many of these tanks took part during the winter defence by the Soviets in front of Leningrad with many either developing mechanical problems or being lost by anti-tank or Panzer fire.

The crew of a Pz.Kpfw.38(t) have halted during their drive towards Leningrad. The distances in which the Panzerwaffe had to travel were immense and supply lines were constantly being overstretched, especially by advanced units spearheading far in front of the advancing column.

Chapter Two

Battles 1942–43

By early 1942 some ten German divisions were tied down around the city of Leningrad. Over the coming weeks and months, the siege of Leningrad continued with Soviet forces constantly attempting to break the German blockade and simultaneously trying to supply the civilian population trapped inside the city. During this time, the Soviets launched a number of offensives to lift the siege, including the Lyuban Offensive which was launched between 7 January and 30 April 1942. No tanks were used in this offensive due to the terrain. However, the attacking Russian forces found themselves under intense German bombardment and were unable to break the German strength due to the lack of artillery support and armour. Consequently, the offensive stalled and the Russians once again went over to the defensive.

Both the Russian Volkhov and Leningrad Fronts lacked armoured vehicles, artillery, ammunition and manpower to mount a sustained offensive against the German 18th Army. When the weather improved by the spring and early summer of 1942, Soviet forces begun launching numerous attacks against the German front but were often annihilated by heavy artillery or Panzer fire.

Following a year-long battle for Leningrad, Hitler ordered a final assault on the besieged city. Army Group North's main objective was to capture Leningrad using thousands of troops supported by artillery and armoured vehicles. The attack was known as Operation Nordlicht or Northern Light. The plan was organized at the same time as preparations for the attack on Stalingrad in the south. Hitler wanted to synchronize the attacks simultaneously to confuse the Russian Army.

Operation Nordlicht was to be launched on 23 August 1942, which would begin with a systematic bombardment of Leningrad followed by a massive aerial attack by the Luftwaffe. However, on 19 August the Russians launched another offensive called the Sinyavino Offensive, which consequently drew off the forces intended to be used in Operation Nordlicht. The German offensive was reluctantly cancelled so forces could concentrate on crushing the Soviet offensive.

The Sinyavino Offensive had actually begun the previous summer. Its aim was to establish a reliable supply line to Leningrad, but due to German strength, the offensive had failed. However, the renewed offensive began in two stages. The Leningrad Front began its offensive on 19 August and the Volkhov Front launched the main attack on 27 August. Initial German attacks to stem the Russian operation failed. Following ten days of fierce fighting, the Germans were able to significantly reinforce its units with heavier artillery and more tanks for the 12th Panzer Division. For four weeks, German forces fought a series of heavy, unrelenting battles to hold their positions around Leningrad. The Germans immediately launched a counteroffensive which saw the first deployment of the new Tiger tanks, but these made only limited gains against overwhelming enemy attacks. Although strong German units held grimly to their lines and managed to blunt Russian penetrations, the losses were immense. By late September, the German forces managed to link up and cut off the bulge formed by the Soviet offensive. Fighting continued until 15 October.

Although the Germans had been successful, the battle had absorbed all the available resources of the 18th Army and elements of the 11th. It had also resulted in the planned assault on Leningrad being completely abandoned. By this point, thousands of the German troops had been killed, and by mid-October 1942, they found themselves substantially in the same position as they had been in the spring of that year. Because of the defeats in southern Russia, German forces were now compelled to go over to the offensive against growing resistance. Despite the prevailing conditions and the daily shelling, Leningrad itself gradually regained strength and became a strong fortress, capable of withstanding a further year and a half of siege.

From the Volkhov River to the Gulf of Finland the front was reminiscent of the First World War – with a string of trenches and shell holes in which gains and losses could be measured only in yards. Because of defeats in southern Russia, German forces were now compelled to go on the defensive against growing resistance. Costly as the Leningrad defence was, it managed to pin down huge parts of Army Group North that were desperately needed elsewhere to plug the crumbling front. When news of the Red Army's breakthrough came on 18 January 1943, it was greeted by soldiers of Army Group North with trepidation. From their relatively inactive front, they watched anxiously as the Russians began increasing their attacks. Commanders in the field were well-aware that if the hold on Leningrad were broken, Army Group North would eventually lose control of the Baltic Sea. Finland would be isolated; supplies of iron ore from Sweden would be in danger, and the U-boat training programme would be seriously curtailed. It was now imperative that the troops held the front and wage a static battle of attrition until other parts of the Russian front could be stabilized.

By the summer of 1943, the front continued to hold. The front-line German strength in July was 710,000 men. Army Group North was also building up a huge number of reserves echeloned in depth behind the northern fronts in the Baltic states of Estonia and Latvia. Both the Germans and Soviets in northern Russia were almost equal in strength, but the Red Army was known to have substantial reserves. They were also building up significant forces to weaken Army Group North's defensive battles around Leningrad and Nevel. The Germans tried their best to hold the lines by shifting Luftwaffe field divisions and SS units newly recruited in the Baltic States.

A Luftwaffe FlaK crew can be seen with their flak gun on tow during winter operations in early 1942.

A knocked out T-34 which has been destroyed during defensive operations on the Leningrad Front.

(**Above**) Winter clad German troops belonging to the 18th Army 262nd Regiment Ski Company supported by a Pz.Kpfw.II during a reconnaissance mission on the Leningrad Front.

(**Opposite, above**) A T-34 belonging to the 30th Guards Tank Brigade of the 67th Army of the Leningrad Front enters Krasnoye Selo.

(**Opposite, below**) A whitewashed Pz.Kpfw.IV has halted outside a town next to a stream during winter operations in early 1942.

(**Opposite, above**) During winter operations and a crewman can be seen in the side escape hatch of a Pz.Kpfw.IV.

(**Opposite, below**) The crew of a stationary Pz.Kpfw.IV can be seen inside a town during operations on the Leningrad Front. Note that all the crew are wearing the standard infantryman's greatcoat due to the lack of proper winter gear.

(**Above**) A Pz.Kpfw.I and crew can be seen posing for the camera. It's quite apparent how unsuited these tankmen are for winter warfare on the Eastern Front. The Pz.Kpfw.I too has not been camouflaged and still retains the standard factory grey paint.

A column of Pz.Kpfw.IIIs on a road. Panzer crews were constantly hampered by the boggy terrain on the Northern Front. As a result, crews often stowed felled wood in order to lay them on parts of the road to avoid the Panzers from becoming stuck.

A halftrack approaches a river hauling a 15cm field howitzer. This weapon was the standard piece in a division and employment of artillery was a necessity to any ground force engaging an enemy. Both infantry and motorized artillery regiments became the backbone of the fighting in the early years on the Russian front.

Finnish tank crew with their T-28 multi-turreted tank. The tank was captured from the Red Army and pressed into service by the Finns to support German forces on Leningrad Front. A large swastika has been painted on the side of turret for recognition purposes. *(SA-Kuva)*

An Sd.Kfz.10/4 mounting a 2cm FlaK 30 gun can be seen in action against what appears to be a ground target. The sides of the halftrack are folded up with additional magazine cases attached. These sides could be folded down to allow extra space on board the halftrack for the flak crew.

Sd.Kfz.251 and Sd.Kfz.250 halftracks can be seen advancing along the side of a rail line. The Sd.Kfz.250 was designed to provide armoured reconnaissance troops to the Panzer and Panzergrenadier divisions with a flexible armoured vehicle that possessed better off road capability than the Sd.Kfz.222 armoured cars.

This Sd.Kfz.7 is pulling an 8.8cm FlaK 18 on a Sd.Ah.201 limber. The vehicle has rod style grab handles mounted between the row of seats to allow quick mounting and dismounting by the crew.

An Sd.Kfz.10/4 halftrack has halted in a field. The sides of the gun platform have been lowered and the crew are heavily embroiled in action against an enemy target. The photograph illustrates just how cramped conditions could be for the crew whilst travelling and during a fire mission.

FlaK gunners with their shielded 2cm Flakvierling 38. These quadruple-barrelled self-propelled anti-aircraft guns demonstrated outstanding anti-aircraft capabilities even during the last months of the war. By this period of operations in the east many of these weapons were being used against Russian heavy armour, which was also very effective.

Soviet KV-1 tanks on parade at the Palace Square in Leningrad in May 1942. These tanks were destined for the Leningrad Front.

Two Sd.Kfz.7/1 halftracks armed with the quadruple 2cm gun FlaK 38 lead a column of vehicles along a winding road during summer operations. The crew have applied foliage to parts of the vehicle to break up its distinctive shape and reduce the possibility of it being attacked by aircraft.

An Sd.Kfz.251 armoured personnel carrier advances through a village. It was primarily the success of the Sd.Kfz.251 in the early war years that afforded halftracks a frontline combat role alongside the Panzer on the Eastern Front.

First Tigers arrive at Mga Station on the Leningrad Front on 29 August 1942, which has caused quite a crowd. These vehicles were deployed by Heavy Tank Battalion 502. The battalion had received their first four Tigers on 19 and 20 August, allowing the Battalion's 1st Company to be formed. Hitler ordered that the Tiger should be used in combat as soon as possible, so despite technical issues, the Company entrained for the Leningrad Front on the 23rd. At full strength, the new battalion would have had nine Tigers and ten Pz.Kpfw.IIIs, but it appears that just four of each were sent. On the day the battalion arrived south-east of Leningrad it saw the first use of the Tiger in combat. However, it was an ominous start. The commander of the 502nd, Major Richard Märker, had advised against deploying the Tigers. Their initial deployment was not successful, with many of the tanks experiencing mechanical breakdowns.

A Horch vehicle crosses a pontoon bridge on the Leningrad Front. This Wehrmacht armoured car was an all-terrain armoured personnel vehicle and was even used as a light artillery tractor.

A Pz.Kpfw.III has been destroyed by enemy anti-tank fire and sits derelict at the side of a forest road.

A stationary Pz.Kpfw.IV has halted on a muddy road in front of a large column of captured Russian soldiers.

An Sd.Kfz.7 advances along a road with a small complement of crew. The canvas foul weather cover has been partially removed so that it allows easy access for the crew to quickly board and dismount and allow all round visibility under battlefield conditions.

Wehrmacht personnel can be seen inside an Sd.Kfz.7, which is hauling an s.FH 18 heavy field howitzer. During the campaign on the Leningrad Front the halftrack transformed the fighting quality of the artillery batteries and enabled gun crews to support the advancing armoured spearheads with less difficulty than using draught animals.

An Sd.Kfz.250 crosses a bridge. There were twelve different variants of the Sd.Kfz.250 series of halftracks, two of which were issued to the Sturmgeschütz units. One of them carried ammunition, known officially as the Sd.Kfz.252, and the other was a battery command and observation vehicle, known as the Sd.Kfz.253.

A Tiger of the 502nd Heavy Panzer Battalion near Leningrad in September or October 1942. Note the Mammoth insignia painted on the rear of the turret. The battalion comprised of just four Tigers, which had minimal impact on the battlefield, and operations in 1942 turned out to be a complete failure. On two of the Tigers, thick mud built up between the interleaved road wheels and consequently overstressed the power train and caused transmission failure. A third suffered engine failure.

A Tiger belonging to the Heavy Tank Battalion 502 on the advance on the Leningrad Front in September 1942. Due to the size of the Tiger, the terrain was not well-suited to this 56-ton vehicle. Vast parts of the Leningrad Front were heavily forested with poor drainage. Consequently, this resulted in large, soft bogs. The heavy rains common at this time of year made matters worse. The battalion fought south of Lake Ladoga near Leningrad but became bogged down in mud.

A whitewashed Pz.Kpfw.III Ausf.J belonging to the 12th Panzer Division. This upgrade variant looked much like the Pz.Kpfw.III Ausf.G. It was designed with a turret housing a 5cm Kampfwagenkanone (KwK) 38 L/42 tank gun. The hull frontal basic armour's thickness had increased to 50mm. An additional armour plate was installed internally to the front of the turret in the spring of 1941, increasing it to a maximum thickness of 57mm in places. Note behind the Ausf.J, is a stationary Horch 108 Type 1 Kfz.21 armoured personnel car.

A stationary whitewashed Tiger tank in the snow belonging to the 502nd Heavy Panzer Battalion. On 14 January 1943, Soviet troops disabled and captured one of the battalion's Tiger tanks during Operation Spark near Leningrad. Operation Spark was a Russian military operation aimed to break the Wehrmacht's siege of Leningrad. The operation was conducted by the Red Army's Leningrad Front, Volkhov Front, and the Baltic Fleet from 12 to 30 January 1943. Its main objective was to create a land connection to Leningrad.

Tiger tank of 502nd Heavy Panzer Battalion on the Leningrad Front in the winter of late 1942 / early 1943. During the initial deployment of the Tiger on the Leningrad Front, the majority of Tiger crewmen were drawn from existing Panzer units. This meant they were well-trained and experienced, but they were new to the different tactics to be used by the Heavy Tank Battalions. Unfortunately, when these Tigers entered operations, there were very few Tiger crews able to successful score considerable successes due to the lack of tactical training.

This photograph was taken on 18 January 1943 on the Volkhov and Leningrad Fronts showing a Tiger tank belonging to the 502nd Heavy Panzer Battalion.

Tiger I belonging to the 502nd Heavy Panzer Battalion stationary on a snowy road in January 1943.

A Tiger tank halted in the snow. Note the smoke candle dischargers attached to the turret sides.

A column of Pz.Kpfw.IIIs crosses a snowy field bound for the front lines in late 1942 or early 1943.

The crew of a whitewashed Pz.Kpfw.III stand in front of their vehicle. The Pz.Kpfw.III saw extensive action in Army Group North. The Ausf.L variant was issued to 502nd Heavy Panzer Battalion alongside Tiger Is, and the unit's first taste of combat was in the Leningrad region from August 1942.

Three personnel, probably part of a heavy artillery unit pose for the camera in front of their Sd.Kfz.7 prime mover in the snow in early January 1943.

A Pz.Kpfw.III Ausf. L, nicknamed 'Luchs' or 'Lynx', entered service in the autumn of 1942 and operated in armoured reconnaissance detachments or Panzer-Aufklarung-Abteilung which were made up of four platoons of seven Luchs and one in the company HQ.

(**Above**) The crew of a Russian T-34 are rearming their tank for offensive action against German positions in an attempt to establish a link with the city of Leningrad.

(**Opposite, above**) A StuG has pulled alongside an Sd.Kfz.250 probably to be resupplied with ammunition during the summer of 1943.

(**Opposite, below**) A Wehrmacht soldier raises his arm to order the launch of rockets from the Panzerwerfer 42 Maultier Sd.Kfz.4/1. These vehicles went into production in April 1943. The rocket launcher was on a chassis referred to as Maultier, which means Mule.

Wehrmacht troops can be seen advancing across a field armed with their Karbiner 98K infantryman's bolt action rifle. Strewn in front of the soldiers are knocked out T-34 tanks that have evidently been destroyed by German anti-tank fire.

A camouflaged Tiger tank and two German crew members from the 502nd Heavy Panzer Battalion on the Leningrad front in August 1943.

A Tiger I heavy tank of the 502nd near Lake Ladoga, August 1943. It was not until the spring of 1943 that the 2nd company of the battalion was formed and fought on the northern sector of the Eastern Front, from Leningrad back through Narva, the Baltic States and then finally East Prussia.

Halted in a field are Sd.Kfz.251 halftracks and a Pz.Kpfw.IV. These vehicles belong to the 12th Panzer Division. For the most part of the war, this division remained on the Northern Sector of the Eastern Front, only being pulled for a brief spell in Army Group Centre at Kursk in July 1943.

(**Above**) A soldier assists an injured comrade out of the rear of an Sd.Kfz.251 halftrack and escorts him probably to one of the rear field hospitals for medical aid.

(**Opposite, above**) Panzergrenadiers can be seen hitching a lift onboard a column of Sd.Kfz.251 halftracks. Panzergrenadiers specialised from and in conjunction with infantry fighting vehicles often from armoured troop carriers that were designated to carry mechanized squads into combat.

(**Opposite, below**) An Sd.Kfz.251 is advancing along a dusty road during heavy fighting in what was known as the Russian Mga Offensive operation or what the Germans referred to as the Third Battle of Lake Ladoga. The Soviet offensive which raged between 22 July and 25 September 1943, made very little progress, but did succeed in conquering a considerable part of the Sinyavino Heights.

A Luftwaffe Sd.Kfz.7 can be seen hauling an 8.8cm FlaK gun. During the summer of 1943 the Red Army carried out heavy attacks against elements of the German 18th Army. The planned Russian attacks were to defeat German forces in Mgd area and to the south-west of the Sinyavino Heights.

Numerous armoured vehicles can be seen during an action in the summer of 1943. Sd.Kfz.251 halftracks and Pz.Kpfw.IIs can be identified. By the end of 1942 the Pz.Kpfw.II had been largely removed from front line service and it was used mainly for training and on secondary fronts. However, on the Northern Front, where armour was at a premium some of the older armoured models were still being used for mainly support purposes.

A well camouflaged Flak gun mounted on the Sd.Kfz.10/4 during action on the Leningrad Front in the summer of 1943.

Two winter clad troops pose in front of a stationary whitewashed Tiger complete with smoke candle dischargers. Note the amount of soldiers that have clambered aboard the tank.

A Pz.Kpfw.IV can be seen in a forest area during heavy fighting. The Pz.Kpfw.IV had limited success in marshy and swampy ground in northern Russia and as result, a number of them either developed mechanical issues or were sitting targets to enemy anti-tank gunners.

A Panther tank during operations in late 1943. This tank made its debut at Kursk and in spite of its unreliability the Panther was rushed to the Northern Front. During Kursk the Panther demonstrated its capacity to destroy any Soviet armoured fighting vehicle from long distance and Hitler was eager to transfer a number of them to help prop-up the deteriorating situation on the Leningrad Front.

Maintenance teams can be seen with Panther tanks preparing them for readiness for shipment to Army Group North. Due to the Kursk offensive in the summer of 1943, Army Group North lacked sufficient armour especially heavy tanks like the Tiger and Panther. In fact, by September 1943 the Panzerwaffe had only forty-nine tanks with forty fit for combat. The Russians on the other hand had 209 tanks on the front lines and an estimated 843 in reserve.

A Tiger belonging to the 502nd Heavy Panzer Battalion has halted beside a knocked out KV-1S on the Leningrad Front in September 1943. Over the course of one year, the Red Army launched numerous attacks that forced the Germans onto the defensive. The swampy terrain continued to restrict heavy vehicle movement but enabled the Tiger tank crews to provide excellent defensive support throughout the sector. Because the Red Army did not possess a tank or armoured vehicle capable of defeating the Tigers, except at close range, Tigers dominated the battlefield in the boggy terrain. From 12 January to 31 March 1943, the battalion managed to destroy 160 Soviet tanks and lost six Tigers.

(**Opposite, above**) A Pz.Kpfw.IV Ausf.G from the 12th Panzer Division in Leningrad, during the reduction of the pocket. In spite of the weakening position on the Leningrad Front the front-line strengths of the opposing forces in the Army Group North zone were almost equal. The army group had 710,000 men. The Red Army Leningrad, Volkhov, Northwest, and Kalinin Fronts had 734,000 men. However, it was German armour that seriously required replenishing.

(**Opposite, below**) An Sd.Kfz.7 inside a forest clearing during operations in September 1943. Operating in Army Group North on the Leningrad Front had been difficult for armoured crews. Muddy and impassable roads, difficult terrain for logistics, and Soviet resistance caused numerous problems.

(**Above**) A halftrack hauls a 10.5cm infantry gun along a road during its unit's withdrawal to what was known as the Panther Line. This line comprised of numerous field fortifications which were being constructed. The withdrawal would be undertaken in tactical stages supported by Panzers and assault guns and using the various defensive positions.

Two Sd.Kfz.251 during possible reconnaissance mission drive along a boggy road. With numerous forests, marshes, and rivers it was often difficult for German vehicles to navigate and supply lines to function effectively. The Soviet transport infrastructure was much poorer than in Western Europe, and the German engineers struggled to adapt their railway systems to the Russian gauge. These terrain-related issues, along with logistical problems and the stiffening Soviet resistance played a significant role in the failure of Army Group North to capture Leningrad, as well as the overall German failure to achieve a decisive victory on the Leningrad Front.

Chapter Three

Leningrad–Novgorod Offensive

In early November 1943, the Soviet Army in northern Russia began building up their forces and transported to the Leningrad Front some 30,000 troops, 47 tanks, 400 artillery pieces, 1,400 trucks and 10,000 tons of ammunition and supplies. When Lake Ladoga froze, another 22,000 soldiers, 800 trucks, 140 tanks and 380 guns were sent overland to their assigned attacking positions. When the Russians had completed their shipments, artillery had been positioned along the entire length of the Leningrad, Second Baltic and Volkhov fronts at a concentration of almost 200 guns per mile. The arsenal comprised of 21,600 standard artillery pieces, 1,500 Katyusha rocket guns, and 600 anti-aircraft guns. The total number of Russian soldiers prepared for action was 1,241,000.

As for the German Army, its tactical position on the northern front had become fragile. Soviet forces far outnumbered their German opponents. The German 18th Army was outnumbered by at least 3:1 in divisions, 3:1 in artillery, and 6:1 in tanks, self-propelled artillery, and aircraft. In total, Army Group North had a combined strength of forty infantry divisions, one Panzergrenadier division and two mountain divisions which were ordered to hold a front of approximately 500 miles of heavily forested and largely marshy ground. Also available to the front for emergency were one field training division and three security divisions. The 18th Army totalled twenty-one infantry divisions, which included five old Luftwaffe field divisions. There were no reserves and very little armour other than a motley collection of Pz.Kpfw.IIIs, Pz.Kpfw.IVs, Marders, Wespes, StuGs and supported by Sd.Kfz.251 and Sd.Kfz.10/4 flak guns. There were also Tigers available from the 502nd Heavy Panzer Battalion. From July to September 1943 the unit had been operating around Lake Ladoga and Newel, near Belarus. By November and December 1943, it covered the retreat of German forces from the Leningrad area and held positions around Narva from February to April 1944.

Panther tanks too were rushed to the Northern Front despite their unreliability. In fact, Hitler had ordered in November 1943 that sixty Panthers without engines or transmissions be sent on the Leningrad Front. They were dug in on the opposite bank of the Konstadt, supported by anti-tank guns, MG positions and infantry. Ten Panthers were put in mobile reserve to form the 1st Abt./Pz.Rgt. 29. Two other Abteilungs arrived the same month for the L Army Corps. By December the 1st Abt/Pz.Rgt. 31 arrived along the Leningrad Front.

On 14 January 1944, the German position was made worse when the Red Army launched its winter offensive against the Leningrad and Volkhov Fronts. The offensive was to attack the German Army Group North supported by parts of the 2nd Baltic Front, with the main objective of fully lifting the siege of Leningrad. The Soviet 2nd Shock Army attacked out of the Oranienbaum around 'Yanvar Grom' through a perimeter held by only two old Luftwaffe fied divisions, SS-Gruppenführer Fritz Scholz's 11th SS Panzergrenadier division 'Nordland' and other elements under the command of Obergruppenführer Felix Steiner's III SS Panzer Corps (germanisch). The III SS Panzer Corps comprised of 103rd SS Heavy Panzer Battalion which had been formed in July 1943.

The Russian offensive was fierce and constant, and the Germans were over-whelmed by the Soviet strength. The Volkhov Front's made a series of large sweeping enveloping attacks in order to try and cut-off Army Group North, decimate its positions in front of Leningrad and prevent its forces from escaping through the Baltic States.

General George von Küchler, the new commander of Army Group North, appealed to Hitler for a complete withdrawal due to the weakened state of its forces. Küchler's proposed a plan to move his forces to a new position to its rear that would shorten the front lines and remove the overwhelming Russian threat. The plan known as Operation Blue was for a withdrawal of over 150 miles to the natural defensive barrier formed by the Narva and Velikaya and Lakes Peipus and Pskov. This position, known as the so-called 'Panther Line', comprised of multiple bunkers and fortifications that had been constructed in late 1943. The withdrawal would be undertaken in tactical stages supported by Panzers and assault guns and using the various defensive positions.

Hitler, as anticipated, responded angrily to the withdrawal proposal and pro-hibited all voluntary withdrawals and reserving all decisions to withdraw to himself. What followed was the Russians opening up the Krasnoye Selo–Ropsha Offen-sive and Novgorod–Luga Offensives. In the Luga region, the offensive was so fierce that after a few days of bitter fighting the German 18th Army had incurred more than 50,000 casualties. As a result of the deteriorating situation Hitler reluctantly approved a retreat to the Luga River but directed that the front be held; contact with 16th Army regained, and all gaps in the front closed.

Although the Germans had suffered massive losses they were not destroyed and were still able to slow down the Soviet drive and from breaking across the Panther-Wotan line. This staunch defence allowed German command to move considerable amounts of forces from the 16th Army to the Luga region. Yet despite this strategic move, by 26 January Soviet forces had regained control of the railway line linking Moscow and Leningrad, and Josef Stalin declared that the siege of Leningrad had been raised, and that the German forces had been expelled from the Leningrad region.

Perturbed by Küchler's strategy Hitler blamed the General for forcing his decision to withdraw and lose positions on the Leningrad Front. As a result, Hitler decided to relieve Küchler of his command and replace him on 31 January 1944 with his trouble shooter, Field Marshall Walter Model. It was Model that ordered his 'Shield and Sword' policy, which stated that retreats were intolerable, but only if they paved the way for a counterstroke later. Now temporary commander of Army Group North he was given the awesome task of trying to minimize the extent of the disaster that was about to loom along the Baltic. It was here in the north that Model had the greatest opportunity to display his talents as an improviser. He immediately sent out an order to all commanders in the field that they were not to step backward. They were also to uphold the Führer's demands that troops were to build defence lines where they stood, and fight to the bitter end.

Model was quite aware of the grave situation and was even more conscious that the battle would soon spill over across into the Baltic State of Estonia. He envisaged that it would be along the borders and inside the heartlands of this country that would see some of the bitterest battles on the Eastern Front.

Churchill tanks of the Soviet 49th Guards Heavy Tank Regiment can be seen on the approaches to the city of Leningrad in January 1944.

Winter clad German troops listen to their commanding officer along a defensive position prior to the Soviet offensive in January 1944. By this point, the situation for Army Group North was extremely precarious. Hitler had been reluctant for any withdrawals and to make matters worse, three intact infantry divisions were transferred to reinforce Manstein's Army Group South that was fighting to hold positions in the Ukraine.

A T-34 76 in the action on the Leningrad front in January 1944. The Leningrad–Novgorod strategic offensive was a strategic offensive launched by the Red Army on 14 January 1944. The objective was to attack the German Army Group North by the Soviet Volkhov and Leningrad fronts, along with elements of the 2nd Baltic Front, with the main aim of fully lifting the siege of Leningrad.

A German infantry man stands next to two knocked-out Soviet KV-1 tank. By this period of the war, the KV tank was seriously under gunned and as a result losses were extremely high.

A German horse-drawn infantry column belonging to the 18th trudge through the snow passing a knocked out Soviet T-34 tank. In early January 1944, 18th Army totalled twenty-one infantry divisions, of which five were ex-Luftwaffe field divisions. There were no reserves and very little armour, and divisional frontages were as much as 14.25 miles.

Soviet self-propelled gunners and infantrymen rest next to a SU-122 self-propelled gun in Krasnoye Selo. Red Army strength for the offensive in January 1944 comprised of 550 tanks against 146 German tanks.

A prime mover advances along a road in the snow hauling an 8.8cm FlaK 18 on a Sd.Ah.201 limber. These FlaK guns served well on the Eastern Front and scored considerable success owing to the rapid transportation of the weapons to the front lines.

An interesting photograph showing a column of vehicles comprising of early production model 8-ton Sd.Kfz.7 halftracks and support vehicles. The prime movers are hauling 15cm s.FH 18 howitzers towards the battlefront.

A whitewashed prime mover fords a river during operations in January 1944. Across the German front a number of German divisions fell back under heavy artillery fire while the Soviet air forces bombed and machine gunned all movement.

An SS flak gunner scours the skies for Soviet aircraft. He is standing on the decking of an Sd.Kfz.7/1 which mounts a 2cm quadruple-barrelled anti-aircraft gun. Note the kill markings displayed on the gun shield. This weapon demonstrated outstanding anti-aircraft capabilities. Though these weapons were used in both ground and aerial roles, in an anti-tank function they were not particularly effective against heavy Russian armour.

A flak crew preparing a defensive position in the snow. An Sd.Kfz.10 can be seen mounting a 3.7cm FlaK gun. These deadly guns were much respected by low-flying Russian airmen and were also particularly devastating against light vehicles, as well as troops caught in the open. The weapon also armed a variety of vehicles on self-propelled mounts where they could be moved from one part of the defensive line to another quickly and efficiently.

A German infantryman wearing his standard issue greatcoat stands in the snow surveying derelict Russian armour that has evidently been destroyed in a previous battle on the Leningrad Front.

Russian soldiers can be seen with captured Tiger tanks at Volosovo, southwest of Leningrad, in January 1944. These Tigers belonged to the 502nd Heavy Panzer Battalion which had been operating around Lake Ladoga from July to September 1943 and Newel, near Belarus during November and December 1943 covering the retreat of German forces from the Leningrad area in January 1944.

On the Leningrad Front in January 1944 Red Army soldiers can be seen with a captured Panther Pz.Kpfw.V Ausf.D.

A Panther tank knocked out during the Red Army offensive in January 1944. Heavy tanks like the Panther and Tiger often supported and defended withdrawing forces, but quite regularly were lost in action as a consequence.

A variety of armoured vehicles comprising of Sd.Kfz.251 halftracks and late variant Pz.Kpfw.IVs can be seen passing through a village during the unit's withdrawal from the Leningrad Front towards Narva.

German infantry can be seen with a whitewashed Sd.Kfz.250 halftrack. By 26 January German troops had been pushed some eighty miles away from the city of Leningrad, and the Moscow-Leningrad rail line had been reopened allowing more suppliers and troops to be sent to the north.

Sd.Kfz.251 halftracks and Pz.Kpfw.IVs can be seen withdrawing through a forest area in January or February 1944. Even by the end of January 1944, Army Group North was not destroyed and was still capable of resisting and causing considerable damage to its enemy.

Winter-clad German infantry use a destroyed Soviet T-34 as cover against enemy fire. By 15 February, Soviet units of the Volkhov Front, as well as the 42nd and 67th Army of the Leningrad Front, reached Lake Peipus, having pushed German formations to the west up to 100-miles in some sectors.

An interesting photograph showing some of the difficulties armoured crews had to face operating in swampy terrain. Felled logs are being laid to allow a Raupenschlepper Ost or Caterpillar Tractor East, more commonly abbreviated as an RSO to move across unhindered. This vehicle was a fully-tracked light weight vehicle designed as a prime mover and artillery supply vehicle. It eventually served in a wide variety of roles.

Tankers of the 222nd separate tank Regiment of the 2nd Shock Army of the Leningrad Front on Karl Marx Avenue in the liberated town of Kingisepp on 1 February 1944.

Winter clad Luftwaffe flak gunners using an 8.8cm Flak gun during a fire mission against a ground target in a defensive position as its unit slowly withdraws towards Narva in February 1944. By this period of the fighting, German units began disintegrating, and in some of the infantry divisions nearly all the regimental and battalion commanders were killed or wounded.

Wehrmacht soldiers pose for the camera in front of their prime mover west of Krasnoye Selo. According to the Soviets, by 30 January the Krasnoye Selo-Ropsha Offensive Operation and Novgorod-Luga Offensive Operation had cost the Germans 21,000 casualties and 85 pieces of artillery. They also lost numerous armour, including assault guns, halftracks and heavy panzers.

Two photographs show knocked-out T-34s in the snow near the town of Luga. Around the town, the Germans defended their positions well and managed to temporarily halt the Soviet advance. However, the German situation on the battlefield was spiralling out of control, and Hitler finally conceded and agreed to the withdrawal of Army Group North to the Panther-Line defences in Estonia and Latvia.

A T-34 76 model 1942 rolls through the city in Leningrad in the early Spring of 1944 following the lift of the siege.

A Pz.Kpfw.IV has been destroyed during its unit's withdrawal in March 1944. By the first half of February, Soviet forces seized control of most of the eastern shore of Lake Peipus and established a number of bridgeheads on the western bank of the Narva River. Much of the area west of the Narva comprised of the III SS Panzer Corps which were ordered to dig defences. It comprised, for the most part, ex-Luftwaffe field divisions and SS volunteer ethnic formations consisting of the 4th SS-Freiwilligen Panzergrenadierbrigade Nederland and 11th SS-Freiwilligen Panzergrenadierdivision Nordland.

Aftermath

Following the German withdrawal of Army Group North from the Leningrad area, troops of the Volkhov Front, as well as the 42nd and 67th Army of the Leningrad Front, advanced at speed towards Lake Peipus, having pushed German forces some 40–100 miles to the West. In total 779 cities and settlements were liberated by the Red Army, including Novgorod, Luga, Batetsky, Oredezh, Mga, Tosno, and Chudovo. What followed was another Soviet offensive known as the Kingisepp-Gdov offensive campaign between the Soviet Leningrad Front and the German 18th Army which was defending positions along the eastern coast of Lake Peipus and the western banks of the Narva River.

On 2 February 1944, Field Marshal Walter Model inspected the front and watched as his divisions were pulled back to the west bank of the Narva River in order to strengthen the city of Narva. Model was totally aware of the geographical significance of Narva and its river line, which acted as a natural obstacle. Following its withdrawal from the Leningrad Front the Germans had established quite a large and strongly defended bridgehead covering an area of territory on the eastern approaches to Narva. The Russians were determined to secure a bridgehead, and Model knew that his force would have to defend the river and the city to the bitter end to prevent the Soviets breaking west and spilling over into the heartlands of Estonia. For this reason, the Narva Front would have to be strengthened with the greatest possible speed if it was going to avert a complete catastrophe in the area. Model was determined to avoid another disaster such as his forces had incurred in front of Leningrad. Hardened soldiers from the SS Division Nordland and Brigade Nederland dug in and were supported by armoured vehicles of the III (Germanic) SS Panzer Corps. All available reserves were to be rushed to the front line, and this included the release of an Estonian brigade.

The Narva was held by a mixture of well-armed and determined soldiers eager not to give an inch to their hated foe. For a number of days, a stalemate of sorts reigned along the river with both sides shelling each other's positions. In spite of the dogged resistance by both German and foreign conscripts, on 6 March the Russians began directing their might against Narva along the main road to Tallinn.

In the smouldering city of Narva, the Germans continued resisting. Soviet air attacks and mercilessly pounded Narva whilst artillery from the 2nd Shock Army launched a fierce unremitting attack firing some 100,000 shells and grenades at three weakened German regiments defending the city. The Nederland Brigade took the brunt of the main attack, but the troops were able to temporarily blunt advance along the river. Two days later, a heavy assault was launched northwest from Narva, bitterly defended by the 4th SS Brigade's 49th Regiment of the SS-Freiwilligen Panzergrenadier-Regiment de Ruyter. For hours, both sides duelled. The fighting was so fierce that the attack disintegrated into violent hand-to-hand battles between advancing Soviet infantry and vastly outnumbered Dutch troops of the 49th SS Regiment. After several hours of fierce combat, the Soviets withdrew with high losses and decided to shift their attack elsewhere.

Over the next two weeks the 4th SS Brigade tried desperately not to fall back, in spite being subjected to constant artillery and air attacks. In other parts of the front the 24th SS Regiment Danmark of the 11th SS Division also received a heavy mauling along with the 4th SS Brigade's 48th Regiment positioned to the south of the 24th SS Regiment. Fighting was very intense and losses were massive resulting in the virtual annihilation of the 49th Regiment's 5th Company.

As parts of the German front began to crumble, the Russian Second Baltic Front stepped up its pressure against the divisions of the 16th Army, trying to punch a hole through its lines. Luckily for the Germans, the weather had turned for the worst. After a warm winter, the spring thaw had set in early. A foot of water covered the ice on the surrounding lakes and Soviet tanks were sometimes sinking up to their turrets. In several places, the roads were turned into a quagmire, making the advance painfully slow.

The Soviet setback enabled Model to quickly improvise, but as he set about increasing the defences on the Narva Front, Hitler transferred his 'trouble shooter' to be commander of Army Group South. General George Lindemann was appointed as acting commanding General of Army Group North. Lindemann was no defence expert, but he soon rallied his commanders in the field to ensure that the front held at all costs.

In the last week of March, Lindemann's dogged determination and fearless attitude saw the Wehrmacht gain the initiative. After seven long weeks of fighting, the Soviet 2nd Shock Army were exhausted, low on supplies, and had suffered too many casualties to enable them to mount any large-scale operations. Consequently, the Russian drive halted and the front line stagnated. With the Russian advance almost coming to a grinding halt, Hitler sent a Fortified Area Order to his front-line commanders. It read:

Hitler's Fortified Area Order March 1944

The Führer   Führer Headquarters
High Command of the Army   8th March 1944
Führer Order No. 11

(Commandants of Fortified Areas and Battle Commandants) In view of various incidents, I issue the following orders:

1. A distinction will be made between 'Fortified Areas', each under a 'Fortified Area Commandant', and 'Local Strong points', each under a 'Battle Commandant'. The 'Fortified Areas' will fulfil the functions of fortresses in

former historical times. They will ensure that the enemy does not occupy these areas of decisive operational importance. They will allow themselves to be surrounded, thereby holding down the largest possible number of enemy forces and establishing conditions for successful counterattacks. Local strong points deep in the battle area will be tenaciously defended in the event of enemy penetrations. By being included in the main line of battle they will act as a reserve of defence and, should the enemy break through, as hinges and cornerstones for the front, forming positions from which counterattacks can be launched.

2. Each 'Fortified Area Commandant' should be a specially selected, hardened soldier, preferably of General's rank. The Army Group concerned will appoint him. Fortified Area commandants will be instructed to personally be responsible to the Commander-in-Chief of the Army Group. Fortified Area Commandants will pledge their honour as soldiers to carry out their duties to the last. Only the Commander-in-Chief of an Army Group in person may, with my approval, relieve the Fortified Area commandant duties, and perhaps order the surrender of the fortified area. Fortified Area Commandants are subordinate to the Commander of the Army Group, or Army, in whose sector the fortified area is situated. Further delegation of command to General officers commanding formations will not take place. Apart from the garrison and its security forces, all persons within a fortified area, or who have been collected there, are under the orders of the commandant, irrespective of whether they are soldiers or civilians, and without regard to their rank or appointment. The Fortified Area Commandant has the military rights and disciplinary powers of a commanding General. In the performance of duties, he will have at his disposal mobile courts-martial and civilian courts. The Army Group concerned will appoint the staff of Fortified Area Commandants. The Chiefs of staff will be appointed by High Command of the Army, in accordance with suggestions made by the Army Group.

3. The Garrison of a fortified area comprises: the security garrison, and the general garrison. The security garrison must be inside the fortified area at all times. Its strength will be laid down by Commander-in-Chief Army Group and will be determined by the size of the area and the tasks to be fulfilled (preparation and completion of defences, holding the fortified area against raids or local attacks by the enemy). The general garrison must be made available to the Commandant of the fortified area in sufficient time for the men to have taken up defensive positions and be installed when a full-scale enemy threatens. Its strength will be laid down by the Commander-in-Chief Army Group, in accordance with the size of the fortified area and the task which is to be performed (total defence of the fortified area).

Signed: ADOLF HITLER

Despite Hitler's directive, the Leningrad Front had been lost forever including considerable ground west of the city. Army Group North were unable to avert the deteriorating situation for any appreciable length of time despite a formidable defensive line. For the next several weeks the Narva Front was held, but this was due to the fact that the Red Army was building up their reserves for a new offensive. The Germans too continued attempting to bring additional reinforcements to the area to try and contain itself cohesively on the battlefield. Although the temporary lull had given the Germans time to build a number of new defensive positions, Army Group North were now exposed by an even greater problem. On 22 June 1944, the Russians launched their long-awaited summer offensive against Army Group Centre, code named Operation Bagration. Within a matter of weeks 17 German divisions had been destroyed. The Soviet attack was so swift that by early July, the 1st Baltic Front was now driving towards Baranovichi and then Molodechno and on to Vilnius, the capital of the Baltic State of Lithuania. What followed was the Battle of Baltics where Army Group North, just three years earlier, had triumphantly conquered Lithuania, Latvia, and Estonia. Its forces had boldly and swiftly spearheaded its powerful forces towards the city of Leningrad. Now in the summer of 1944, it was bitterly contesting every foot of ground, trying in vain to maintain its positions against overwhelming enemy strength whilst slowly and remorselessly withdrawing.

Waffen-SS troops hitch a lift onboard an Sd.Kfz.10 during its unit's withdrawal west of the Narva River. Over the coming weeks, Soviet forces of the Volkhov and Leningrad Fronts began exerting more pressure, especially against the 16th Army that was defending positions along the Baltic. But thankfully for the Germans, the spring thaw had arrived early. Melting snow had turned the roads on which the Russians were travelling into a quagmire.

German troops rest at the side of the road in a ditch. In the distance, German armoured vehicles can be seen on the move. By the middle of February, the situation on the Narva front was catastrophic for Army Group North. The Leningrad Front had established bridgeheads both to the north and to the south of Narva.

Winter-clad infantry protect themselves from enemy fire behind a whitewashed Tiger in February 1944. In order to defend Narva, a formation was put together known as 'Detachment Narva'. The commander put in charge of its defence was SS-Obergruppenführer Felix Steiner. His detachment comprised of the III SS Panzer Corps which contained mostly SS volunteer formations like Nordland, Nederland and Estonian. There were even Estonian police battalions drafted into the defence and supported by the 502nd Heavy Tank Battalion.

SS-Gruppen Führer Strachwitz can be seen observing his troops unloading supplies from an Sd.Kfz.251 halftrack in March 1944. His men nicknamed him as the 'Der Panzergraf' and he commanded a battle group known as Kampfgruppe Strachwitz which comprised of the 170th, 11th, and 227th Infantry Division and a tank hunting brigade. *(Bundesarchiv Bild 101I-701-0357-17)*

Two photographs showing SS-Gruppen Führer Strachwitz who was awarded the Swords to his Knight's Cross on 28 March 1944. His soldiers honoured him for his bravery and leadership by changing the popular song 'Lutzow' for 'Lutzow's Wild'. This change in the popular song was a form of recognition and admiration for the Panzer leader, reflecting his impact on the unit.

(Lower image: Bundesarchiv Bild-101I-701-0357-14)

Strachwitz in the cupola of a panzer. On 1 April 1944, Strachwitz had been promoted to SS-Gruppen Führer, and appointed commander of the 1st Panzer Division. Shortly thereafter, he was appointed Higher Panzer Leader of Army Group North with three Panzer divisions and a Panzerbrigade. In early 1945, he was once again promoted to SS-Obergruppenführer.

A Tiger belonging to the 502nd Heavy Panzer Battalion can be seen operating in the snow probably in February 1944. The battalion went on to defend positions around Narva in late March under the command of the 'panzer ace' Otto Carius.

'Panzer ace' Otto Carius dressed in his Army (Heer) summer white dress tunic. He was given the command of the 502nd Heavy Panzer Battalion in March 1944. Oberleutnant von Schiller was officially in command but lacked the respect of the rest of the company. Von Schiller was only too pleased to allow Carius the task of commanding the Tiger Company and defending Narva.

(Bundesarchiv Bild 146-1979-064-06)

Finnish troops on top of a T-34 destroyed by a Panzerschreck. The penetrating hit can be seen below the tactical number '1' painted on the side of the turret in the early summer of 1944.

A completely wrecked Tiger knocked out of action during a defensive action against powerful units of the Red Army 2nd Baltic Front.

A decimated Sd.Kfz.251, testimony to the heavy fighting along the borders of Estonia as the German front receded following the complete collapse of German operations on the Leningrad Front.

Among the wreckage of a number of knocked out Soviet tanks, a Panzergrenadier scours the terrain through a pair of binoculars from a ditch at the side of a road.

Appendix One

German Order of Battle

German Army Group North (Heeresgruppe Nord)
(Field Marshal Wilhelm Ritter von Leeb)

8 August 1941

18th Army (Generaloberst Georg von Küchler)

The XXXXII Army Corps was transferred to the 18th Army on 18 July 1941.

XXXXII Army Corps (Walter Kuntze)
- 61st Infantry Division
- 217th Infantry Division

XXVI Army Corps (Albert Wodrig)
- 93rd Infantry Division
- 291st Infantry Division
- 254th Infantry Division

Panzergruppe 4 (Generaloberst Erich Hoepner)

XXXXI Corps (mot.) (Georg-Hans Reinhardt)
- 1st Infantry Division
- 8th Panzer Division
- 1st Panzer Division
- 36th Infantry Division (mot.)
- 6th Panzer Division

LVI Motorized Corps (Erich von Manstein)
- 269th Infantry Division
- 3rd Infantry Division (mot.)
- SS Polizei Division

XXXVIII Corps (Friedrich-Wilhelm von Chappuis)
- 58th Infantry Division

L Army Corps (Georg Lindemann) (from 14 August 1941)
- 269th Infantry Division
- SS Polizei Division

16th Army (Generaloberst Ernst Busch)

XXVIII Army Corps (Mauritz von Wiktorin)
- 96th Infantry Division
- 122nd Infantry Division
- 121st Infantry Division
- SS Totenkopf Division

I Army Corps (Kuno-Hans von Both)
- 11th Infantry Division
- 126th Infantry Division
- 21st Infantry Division

II Army Corps (Walter von Brockdorff-Ahlefeldt)
- 12th Infantry Division
- 123rd Infantry Division
- 32nd Infantry Division

X Army Corps (Christian Hansen)
- 30th Infantry Division
- 290th Infantry Division

3rd Panzer Group

XXXIX Motorized Corps (Rudolf Schmidt)

    12th Panzer Division   20th Motorized Division
    18th Motorized Division
LVII Motorized Corps (Adolf-Friedrich Kuntzen)
    19th Panzer Division   20th Panzer Division

Luftflotte 1

3 August 1941

2.(F)/ObdL Wekusta (2nd Squadron, Long-Range reconnaissance Luftwaffe High
   Command)
1 KGr z.b.V. 106 (1st Transport Squadron, 106th Military Transport Group)

I. Fliegerkorps

5th Squadron, 122nd Intelligence Group
Kampfgeschwader 1 – He 111H, Ju 88A (Group 2 and 3)
Kampfgeschwader 76 – Ju 88A
Kampfgeschwader 77 – Ju 88A
Sturzkampfgeschwader 77 – Ju 87B, Bf 110
Zerstörergeschwader 26 – Bf 110 (Group 1 and 2)
Jagdgeschwader 54 – Bf 109F
Jagdgeschwader 53 – Bf 109F (Group 2 only)

VIII. Fliegerkorps

The VIII. Fliegerkorps took part in the operation from late July to 20 September
   1941.

2nd Squadron, 11th Intelligence Group
1st Transport Squadron, 4th Transport Group
Kampfgeschwader 2 – Do 17Z (Group 1)
Kampfgeschwader 3 – Do 17Z (Group 3)
Schnellkampfgeschwader 210 – Bf 110 (Group 2)
Sturzkampfgeschwader 2 – Ju 87B (Group 1, 3)
Lehrgeschwader 2 – Bf 109E, Hs-123 (2nd and 10th Squadron)
Jagdgeschwader 27 – Bf 109F, Bf 109E (Group 3 only)
Jagdgeschwader 52 – Bf 109F (Group 2 only)

Soviet Order of Battle 10 July to 23 August 1941

Northern Front Defensive Operations

The Northern Fronts were divided into the Karelian and Leningrad Fronts

1 July 1941

23rd Army (Defending the approaches north of Leningrad)
16th Rifle Division70th Rifle Division
177th Rifle Division
191st Rifle Division
1st Mountain Rifle Brigade
8th Rifle Brigade
Separate Kursantska Rifle Brigade
21st Fortified Region
22nd Fortified Region
12th Engineer Regiment
29th Engineer Regiment

39th Fighter Aviation Division
41st Bomber Aviation Division
1st Mixed Aviation Division
2nd Mixed Aviation Division
3rd Mixed Aviation Division
4th Mixed Aviation Division
5th Mixed Aviation Division
55th Mixed Aviation Division
3rd PVO Fighter Aviation Division
54th PVO Fighter Aviation Division
14th Bomber Aviation Regiment

1st August 1941

11th Army
27th Army
Novgorod Operational Group
5th Airborne Corps
9th Airborne Brigade
10th Airborne Brigade
201st Airborne Brigade
41st Cavalry Division (Forming)
9th Antitank Brigade
10th Antitank Brigade
270th Corps Artillery Regiment
448th Corps Artillery Regiment
110th High-Power Howitzer Artillery Regiment
402nd High-Power Howitzer Artillery Regiment

429th High-Power Howitzer Artillery Regiment (RVGK)
11th Antiaircraft Artillery Battalion
19th Antiaircraft Artillery Battalion
10th PVO Brigade
Riga PVO Brigade Region
Estonian PVO Brigade Region
Kaunas PVO Brigade Region
1st Mechanized Corps
3rd Tank Division
12th Mechanized Corps
23rd Tank Division
28th Tank Division
125th Tank Regiment
25th Engineer Battalion
110th Motorized Engineer Battalion

50th Pontoon-Bridge Battalion
55th Pontoon-Bridge Battalion
56th Pontoon-Bridge Battalion
57th Pontoon-Bridge Battalion

4th Mixed Aviation Division
6th Mixed Aviation Division
57th Mixed Aviation Division

1st September 1941

11th Army
27th Army
34th Army
Novgorod Operational Group
33rd Rifle Division
84th Rifle Division
54th Cavalry Division
310th Rifle Division (under command
    of the North-western direction)
10th Antitank Brigade
402nd High-Power Howitzer Artillery
    Regiment (RVGK)
429th High-Power Howitzer Artillery
    Regiment (RVGK)
171st Antitank Artillery Regiment
759th Antitank Artillery Regiment

19th Antiaircraft Artillery Battalion
111th Antiaircraft Artillery Battalion
239th Antiaircraft Artillery Battalion
246th Antiaircraft Artillery Battalion
250th Antiaircraft Artillery Battalion
Riga PVO Brigade Region
Estonian PVO Brigade Region
Kaunas PVO Brigade Region
34th Motorcycle Regiment
25th Engineer Battalion
50th Pontoon-Bridge Battalion
55th Pontoon-Bridge Battalion
56th Pontoon-Bridge Battalion
57th Pontoon-Bridge Battalion
6th Mixed Aviation Division
415th Fighter Aviation Regiment

1 October 1941

11th Army
27th Army
34th Army
Novgorod Operational Group
25th Cavalry Division
46th Cavalry Division
54th Cavalry Division
10th Antitank Brigade
171st Antitank Artillery Regiment
759th Antitank Artillery Regiment
3rd Guards Mortar Regiment
Riga PVO Brigade Region
Estonian PVO Brigade Region
Kaunas PVO Brigade Region
11th Antiaircraft Artillery Battalion
29th Antiaircraft Artillery Battalion

239th Antiaircraft Artillery Battalion
246th Antiaircraft Artillery Battalion
250th Antiaircraft Artillery Battalion
125th Tank Brigade
87th Tank Battalion
110th Tank Battalion
112 Tank Battalion
112 Tank Battalion
116th Tank Battalion
34th Motorcycle Regiment
57th Pontoon-Bridge Battalion
67th Sapper Battalion
492nd Sapper Battalion
494th Sapper Battalion
6th Mixed Aviation Division

Leningrad People's Militia
Luga Operational Group / Southern Operational Group

1 August 1941

41st Rifle Corps
111th Rifle Division
177th Rifle Division
235th Rifle Division
1st Rifle Regiment (3rd Leningrad
  People's Militia Division)
260th Machine-Gun Artillery Battalion

262nd Machine-Gun Artillery Battalion
541st Howitzer Artillery Regiment
  (RVGK)
Luga PVO Brigade Region
24th Tank Division
259th Sapper Battalion

Kopor Operational Group

September 1941

1st Guards Leningrad People's Militia
  Division
2nd Leningrad People's Militia Division
522nd Rifle Regiment (191st Rifle
  Division)

519th Howitzer Artillery Regiment
  (RVGK)
24th Tank Regiment (1st Tank
  Division)
295th Sapper Battalion

Neva Operational Group

1 October 1941

115th Rifle Division
1st Rifle Division (NKVD)
4th Naval Infantry Brigade
1st Fighter Battalion
4th Fighter Battalion
5th Fighter Battalion
230th Artillery Regiment (71st Rifle
  Division)

1/577th Howitzer Artillery Regiment
24th Antitank Artillery Battalion
20th Mortar Battalion
107th Tank Battalion
21st Pontoon-Bridge Battalion

Novgorod Operational Group

1 August 1941

16th Rifle Corps (HQ used to form
  48th Army on 7 August)
70th Rifle Division
128th Rifle Division

237th Rifle Division
1st Leningrad People's Militia Division
1st Mountain Rifle Brigade
21st Tank Division

1 September 1941

305th Rifle Division
448th Corps Artillery Regiment
Separate Mortar Battalion
8th Antiaircraft Artillery Battalion

3rd Tank Division
28th Tank Division
50th Engineer Battalion

October 1941

180th Rifle Division
185th Rifle Division

305th Rifle Division
Mixed Rifle Regiment

264th Corps Artillery Regiment
448th Corps Artillery Regiment
Mortar Battalion (unnumbered)
8th Antiaircraft Battalion
242nd Antiaircraft Battalion
3rd Tank Division
25th Engineer Battalion
50th Engineer-Bridge Battalion
55th Engineer-Bridge Battalion
56th Engineer-Bridge Battalion

Red Army

1 July 1941

23rd Army (Defending the
  approaches north of Leningrad)
16th Rifle Division
70th Rifle Division
177th Rifle Division
191st Rifle Division
1st Mountain Rifle Brigade
8th Rifle Brigade
Separate Kursantska Rifle Brigade
21st Fortified Region
22nd Fortified Region
12th Engineer Regiment
29th Engineer Regiment
39th Fighter Aviation Division
41st Bomber Aviation Division
1st Mixed Aviation Division
2nd Mixed Aviation Division
3rd Mixed Aviation Division
4th Mixed Aviation Division
5th Mixed Aviation Division
55th Mixed Aviation Division
3rd PVO Fighter Aviation Division
54th PVO Fighter Aviation Division
14th Bomber Aviation Regiment

1 August 1941

11th Army
27th Army
Novgorod Operational Group
5th Airborne Corps
9th Airborne Brigade
10th Airborne Brigade
201st Airborne Brigade
41st Cavalry Division (Forming)
9th Antitank Brigade
10th Antitank Brigade
270th Corps Artillery Regiment
448th Corps Artillery Regiment
110th High-Power Howitzer Artillery
  Regiment
402nd High-Power Howitzer Artillery
  Regiment
429th High-Power Howitzer Artillery
  Regiment (RVGK)
11th Antiaircraft Artillery Battalion
19th Antiaircraft Artillery Battalion
10th PVO Brigade
Riga PVO Brigade Region
Estonian PVO Brigade Region
Kaunas PVO Brigade Region
1st Mechanized Corps
3rd Tank Division
12th Mechanized Corps
23rd Tank Division
28th Tank Division
125th Tank Regiment
25th Engineer Battalion
110th Motorized Engineer Battalion
50th Pontoon-Bridge Battalion
55th Pontoon-Bridge Battalion
56th Pontoon-Bridge Battalion
57th Pontoon-Bridge Battalion
4th Mixed Aviation Division
6th Mixed Aviation Division
57th Mixed Aviation Division

1 September 1941

11th Army
27th Army
34th Army
Novgorod Operational Group
33rd Rifle Division
84th Rifle Division
54th Cavalry Division
310th Rifle Division (Under command
    of the North-western direction)
10th Antitank Brigade
402nd High-Power Howitzer Artillery
    Regiment (RVGK)
429th High-Power Howitzer Artillery
    Regiment (RVGK)
171st Antitank Artillery Regiment
759th Antitank Artillery Regiment

1 October 1941

11th Army
27th Army
34th Army
Novgorod Operational Group
25th Cavalry Division
46th Cavalry Division
54th Cavalry Division
10th Antitank Brigade
171st Antitank Artillery Regiment
759th Antitank Artillery Regiment
3rd Guards Mortar Regiment
Riga PVO Brigade Region
Estonian PVO Brigade Region
Kaunas PVO Brigade Region
11th Antiaircraft Artillery Battalion

19th Antiaircraft Artillery Battalion
111th Antiaircraft Artillery Battalion
239th Antiaircraft Artillery Battalion
246th Antiaircraft Artillery Battalion
250th Antiaircraft Artillery Battalion
Riga PVO Brigade Region
Estonian PVO Brigade Region
Kaunas PVO Brigade Region
34th Motorcycle Regiment
25th Engineer Battalion
50th Pontoon-Bridge Battalion
55th Pontoon-Bridge Battalion
56th Pontoon-Bridge Battalion
57th Pontoon-Bridge Battalion
6th Mixed Aviation Division
415th Fighter Aviation Regiment

29th Antiaircraft Artillery Battalion
239th Antiaircraft Artillery Battalion
246th Antiaircraft Artillery Battalion
250th Antiaircraft Artillery Battalion
125th Tank Brigade
87th Tank Battalion
110th Tank Battalion
112? Tank Battalion (source is unclear)
112? Tank Battalion (source is unclear)
116th Tank Battalion
34th Motorcycle Regiment
57th Pontoon-Bridge Battalion
67th Sapper Battalion
492nd Sapper Battalion
494th Sapper Battalion
6th Mixed Aviation Division

Appendix Three

Order of Battle
February 1943

Soviet Union – Leningrad Front

Soviet 55th Army, 38,000 soldiers
43rd Rifle Division
45th Guards Rifle Division
63rd Guards Rifle Division
122nd Tank Brigade
31st Tank Regiment
34th Ski Brigade
35th Ski Brigade
Artillery and mortar regiments with a total strength of 1,000 guns and mortars

Germany – Army Group North, 18th Army

German 50th Corps
Elements of 250th Infantry Division (Spanish Blue Division)
250 Field Replacement Battalion
262 Regiment (three battalions)
Ski Company
250 Reconnaissance Battalion
1st Artillery Battalion (three Batteries) with 10.5cm guns
One battery of 3rd Artillery Battalion with 10.5cm guns
One battery of 4th Artillery Battalion with 15.0cm guns
250th Anti-Tank Battalion with 3.7cm PaK 36 AT-guns
Assault sappers group
Independent anti-tank gun company with 7.5cm PaK 40 anti-tank guns
4th SS Polizei Division
Battle Group 11th Infantry Division
Battle Group 21st Infantry Division
Battle Group 212th Infantry Division
Battle Group 215th Infantry Division
Battle Group 227th Infantry Division
Battle Group 2nd SS Motorized Brigade
SS-Volunteer Legion Flandern (two companies)